Zarna Garg

Zarna Garg , born circa 1975, is a trailblazing Indian-American stand-up comedian, screenwriter, and podcast host who has emerged as one of the most distinctive voices in modern comedy. Known for her sharp wit, unfiltered humor, and unique perspective on cultural identity, CNBC aptly described her as "the zany, outspoken voice of the Indian American woman."

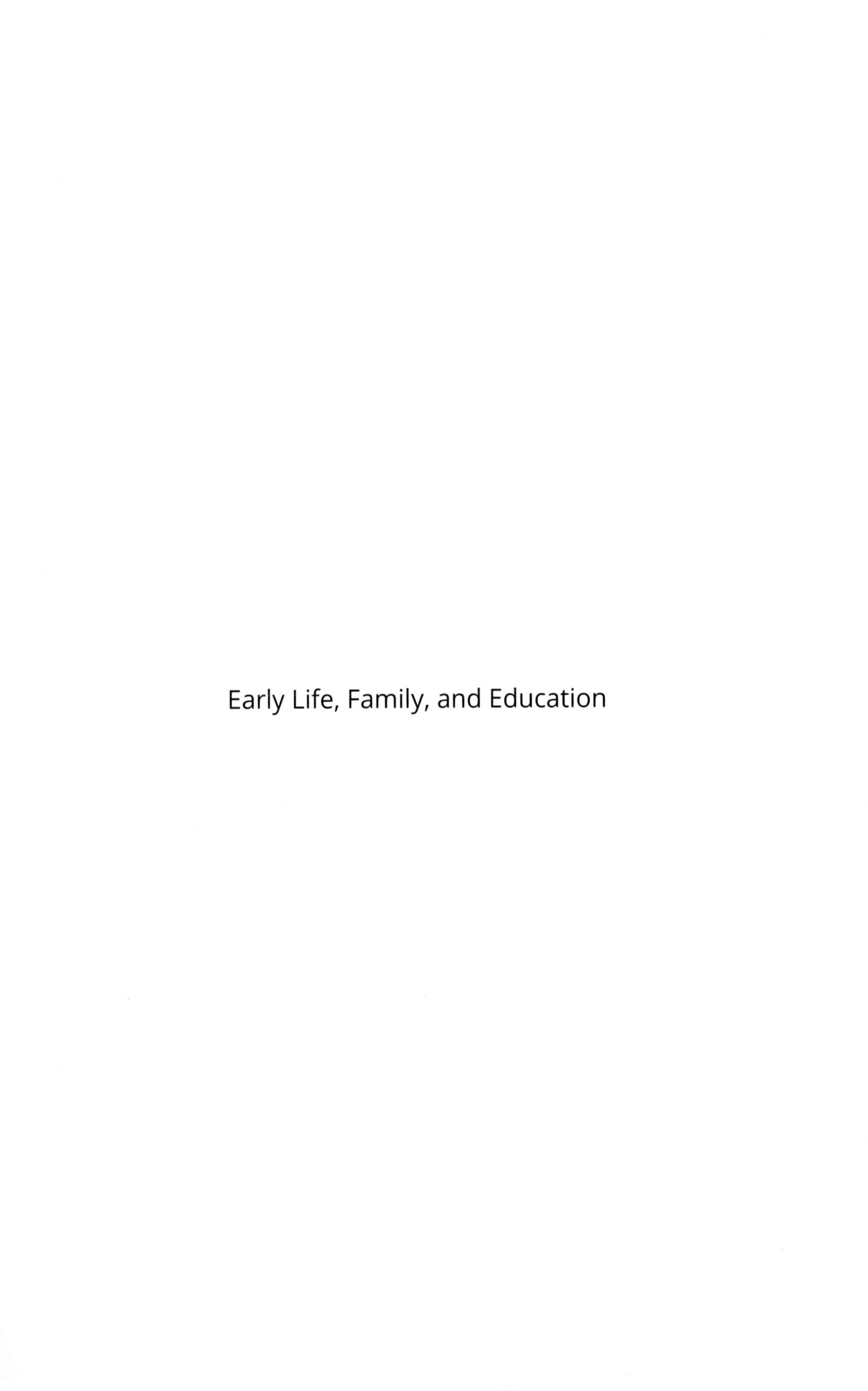

Early Life, Family, and Education

Zarna was born in India and spent her teenage years in Mumbai. Her early life was marked by both tragedy and resilience. At just fourteen years old, she lost her mother to jaundice—a devastating event that would shape her journey profoundly. Following her mother's death, Zarna faced immense pressure from her father to enter into an arranged marriage the very next day. Refusing to conform to societal expectations, she made the bold decision to leave home, finding refuge with friends and extended family.

Determined to forge her own path, Zarna eventually immigrated to the United States, settling in Akron, Ohio, where she lived with her sister. She pursued higher education with unwavering determination, earning a bachelor's degree in finance from the University of Akron and later a Juris Doctor degree from Case Western Reserve University School of Law. Despite her academic achievements, Zarna chose to step back from her professional career to focus on raising her three children, dedicating 16 years to being a stay-at-home mother. It wasn't until her children encouraged her to explore her passion for storytelling that she discovered her true calling—stand-up comedy.

Career Breakthrough

In 2018, at the age of 43, Zarna took her first brave steps onto the stage at an open mic night in New York City. This marked the beginning of an extraordinary career shift. By February 2019, she had landed her first official stand-up performance at the iconic Carolines on Broadway, quickly establishing herself as a rising star in the comedy world.

Her talents extend beyond stand-up; Zarna is also an accomplished screenwriter. Her debut romantic comedy screenplay, Rearranged , earned critical acclaim when it won the Best Comedy Screenplay Award at the prestigious 2019 Austin Film Festival. The script further solidified her reputation as a formidable storyteller by becoming a semi-finalist in the 2019 Academy Nicholl Fellowships competition.

Over the next few years, Zarna continued to make waves in the entertainment industry. In 2021, she claimed victory in Kevin Hart's comedy competition series Lyft Comics on Peacock. That same year, she received the Ladies of Laughter Award in the Newcomer Winner category. Her growing influence led to appearances on major platforms like Tamron Hall, TODAY, and NPR's This American Life , where she shared how her daughter Zoya inspired her comedic journey.

In 2022, Zarna was featured in Apple TV's docuseries Gutsy , hosted by Hillary and Chelsea Clinton, which celebrated her as "one of the gutsiest women comedians in America." Her groundbreaking work culminated in the release of her first comedy special, Zarna Garg: One in a Billion , on Prime Video in May 2023. Filmed at New York City's Gramercy Theatre, the special showcased her quick wit and rapid-fire punchlines, earning praise from critics, including Jason Zinoman of The New York Times , who noted her sitcom-ready presence.

Podcasting and Acting Ventures

Beyond stand-up, Zarna has expanded her creative endeavors through podcasting and acting. She produces and hosts The Zarna Garg Show , a popular family podcast available on platforms like YouTube, Spotify, and Apple Podcasts. The show offers listeners a candid glimpse into her life, blending humor with heartfelt conversations about family dynamics and cultural nuances.

In 2023, Zarna added acting to her résumé with a role in the film A Nice Indian Boy , which premiered at the SXSW Film Festival. Playing the matriarch of the Gavaskar family, she brought authenticity and charm to the screen, delighting audiences with her portrayal.

Her late-night debut came in January 2024 on The Tonight Show Starring Jimmy Fallon , where she delivered a memorable set that resonated with viewers nationwide. Later that year, she joined forces with comedy legends Tina Fey and Amy Poehler, opening for their tour while simultaneously working on her second stand-up hour, Practical People Win . With international dates lined up, Zarna continues to captivate global audiences with her razor-sharp humor and relatable stories.

Personal Life

Zarna's personal life reflects the same courage and independence that define her career. In 1998, she married Shalabh Garg, whom she met online—an unconventional choice at the time. Together, they have three children and reside in New York City. Their story often serves as inspiration for her comedy routines, offering audiences a humorous yet poignant look at love, marriage, and parenthood within an immigrant household.

Legacy and Impact

From overcoming adversity in her youth to breaking barriers in the male-dominated world of comedy, Zarna Garg's journey is a testament to resilience, reinvention, and the power of laughter. As she continues to push boundaries in stand-up, screenwriting, and podcasting, Zarna remains committed to amplifying underrepresented voices and challenging stereotypes. Whether performing on stage, hosting her podcast, or starring in films, she consistently proves that practicality may win—but humor conquers all.

With her infectious energy, fearless authenticity, and undeniable talent, Zarna Garg stands as a beacon of hope and hilarity for aspiring creators everywhere.

Breaking Barriers and Inspiring Others

Zarna Garg's rise in the entertainment industry has been nothing short of meteoric, but her impact extends far beyond laughs. She has become a cultural ambassador for Indian-American women, using humor as a bridge to connect diverse audiences while addressing topics often considered taboo. Her ability to tackle sensitive subjects—such as arranged marriages, generational divides, and the immigrant experience—with both levity and poignancy has earned her widespread acclaim.

Through her work, Zarna challenges societal norms and encourages others to embrace their individuality. Her journey from a stay-at-home mom to a celebrated comedian and screenwriter serves as an inspiring blueprint for anyone hesitant to pursue their dreams later in life. By sharing her vulnerabilities on stage, she reminds us that resilience can be found even in the most unexpected places.

Expanding Creative Horizons

Beyond her stand-up specials and podcasting ventures, Zarna continues to push creative boundaries. In addition to writing Rearranged , which remains one of her proudest accomplishments, she is currently developing new projects that blend comedy with social commentary. Her storytelling reflects not only her personal experiences but also universal themes of love, identity, and belonging.

Her role in A Nice Indian Boy marked just the beginning of her acting career. With her natural charisma and comedic timing, it's no surprise that Hollywood has taken notice. Industry insiders predict more acting opportunities are on the horizon, further cementing her status as a multifaceted entertainer.

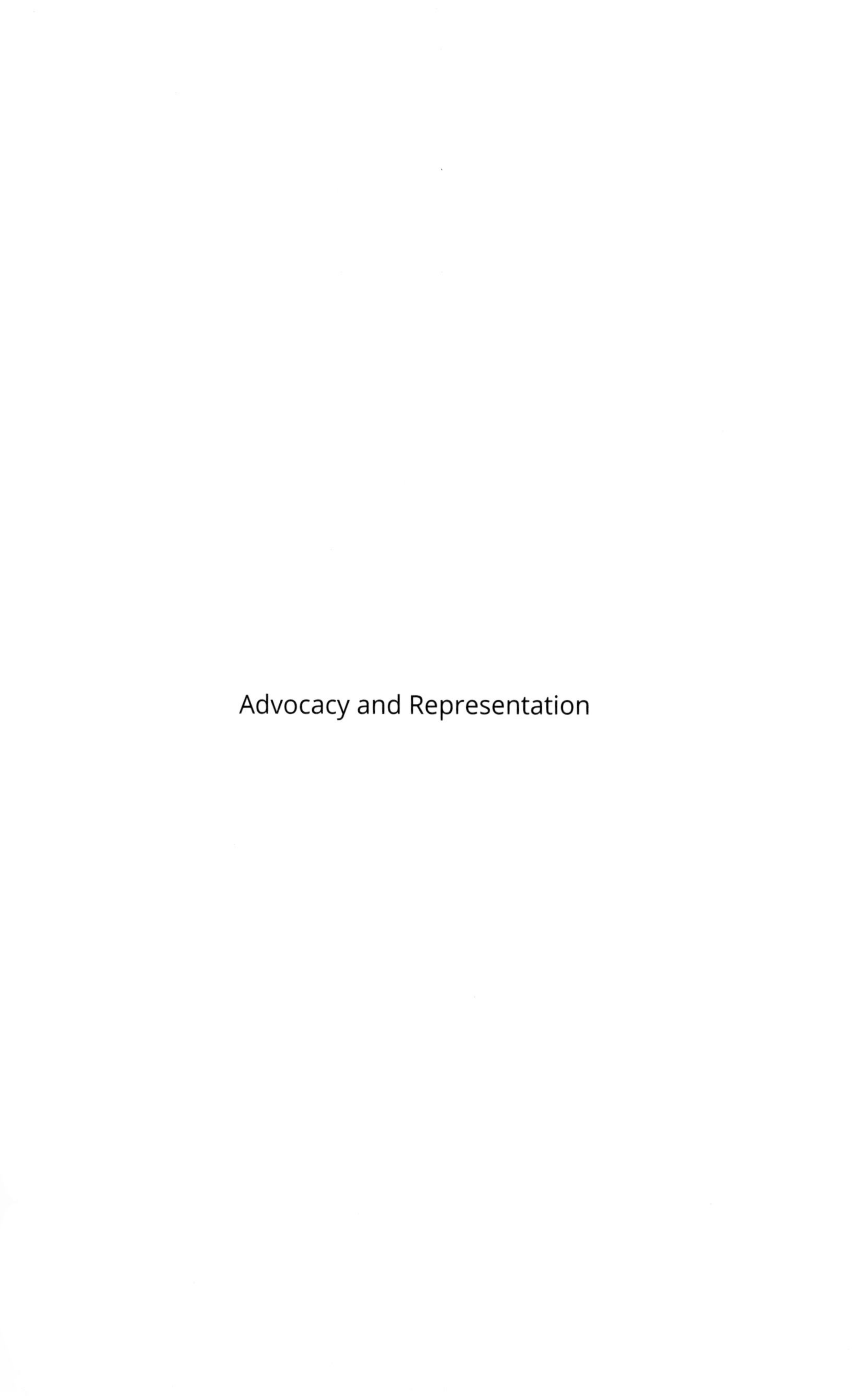

Advocacy and Representation

As a prominent figure in the South Asian community, Zarna uses her platform to advocate for greater representation in media. She frequently speaks about the importance of authentic storytelling and creating space for underrepresented voices. Whether through interviews, public appearances, or her own content, she emphasizes the need for nuanced portrayals of minority communities.

In 2023, Zarna hosted the National Women's History Museum’s Women Making History Awards , where she celebrated trailblazing women who have shattered glass ceilings across various fields. Her involvement underscored her commitment to uplifting others and fostering a culture of inclusivity.

The Power of Family

Central to Zarna's success is her close-knit family, who continue to inspire much of her material. Her husband, Shalabh, often appears alongside her in discussions about their unconventional relationship journey, offering fans a glimpse into their enduring partnership. Meanwhile, her children remain her biggest cheerleaders, having played a pivotal role in encouraging her to pursue comedy in the first place.

The Gargs' dynamic provides rich fodder for Zarna's routines, allowing her to explore themes like parenting, cultural expectations, and the complexities of balancing tradition with modernity. Through her stories, she paints a vivid picture of what it means to navigate dual identities in today's world.

Looking Ahead

With her star continuing to rise, Zarna shows no signs of slowing down. Her upcoming stand-up tour, Practical People Win , promises to deliver her signature blend of humor and heart while delving deeper into the realities of adulthood, relationships, and self-discovery. The tour will take her across the United States and internationally, solidifying her reputation as a global comedic force.

Simultaneously, she plans to expand The Zarna Garg Show by introducing new segments and collaborations, ensuring the podcast remains a vibrant hub for storytelling and connection. Fans eagerly await updates on her next screenplay, rumored to explore themes of family and forgiveness against the backdrop of contemporary America.

A Lasting Legacy

Zarna Garg's story is one of courage, creativity, and connection. From surviving personal hardships to conquering the comedy circuit, she has proven time and again that laughter truly is the best medicine—and sometimes, the strongest weapon against adversity. As she continues to break barriers and redefine what it means to be a woman in comedy, Zarna leaves an indelible mark on the industry and beyond.

Her legacy lies not only in her achievements but also in the countless lives she inspires daily. To her audience, she represents proof that it's never too late to chase your dreams—and that doing so with humor makes the journey all the more rewarding.

Zarna Garg isn't just making history; she's rewriting it, one joke at a time.

Mentorship and Community Engagement

Beyond her performances and creative pursuits, Zarna Garg has emerged as a mentor for aspiring comedians and storytellers. Recognizing the challenges faced by underrepresented voices in entertainment, she actively participates in workshops, panels, and mentorship programs aimed at nurturing the next generation of talent. Her advice often centers around authenticity: "Speak your truth," she says, "because there's always someone out there who needs to hear it."

Zarna also collaborates with organizations that support marginalized communities, including initiatives that promote diversity in media and the arts. Whether through speaking engagements or charitable efforts, she leverages her platform to advocate for systemic change while encouraging individuals to find their own unique voice.

Her involvement extends to educational institutions, where she frequently shares insights from her unconventional career trajectory. She emphasizes the importance of resilience, adaptability, and humor in navigating life's unpredictability—a message that resonates deeply with students and professionals alike.

Global Reach and Cultural Impact

As Zarna's career expands internationally, so does her influence on global audiences. Her comedy transcends cultural barriers, offering universal lessons wrapped in culturally specific anecdotes. Audiences from New York to Mumbai have praised her ability to make them laugh while prompting reflection on shared human experiences.

Her international tours not only showcase her comedic prowess but also serve as opportunities to engage with diverse communities. During these travels, Zarna often immerses herself in local cultures, drawing inspiration for her material while fostering cross-cultural understanding. This global perspective enriches her storytelling, ensuring her work remains relevant and relatable across continents.

In interviews, she speaks candidly about the challenges of balancing her Indian heritage with her American identity, a duality that informs much of her humor. By embracing this complexity, she challenges stereotypes and redefines what it means to be a modern immigrant woman.

Innovations in Storytelling

Zarna's creativity knows no bounds, and she continues to experiment with new formats and mediums to tell her stories. Beyond stand-up and podcasting, she is exploring immersive theater and digital content creation as ways to connect with audiences in innovative ways. Her vision includes interactive experiences that allow fans to engage directly with her narratives, creating a more personal and impactful connection.

She is also working on adapting Rearranged into a feature film, a project that holds special significance given its origins as her award-winning screenplay. With plans to produce and potentially star in the adaptation, Zarna aims to bring her characters to life on the big screen while staying true to the story's heartfelt roots.

Additionally, she has expressed interest in collaborating with other creators—both within and outside the South Asian diaspora—to develop projects that highlight intersectional perspectives. These collaborations reflect her belief in the power of collective storytelling to drive social progress.

Overcoming Challenges with Grace

Despite her success, Zarna's journey has not been without obstacles. Navigating the male-dominated world of comedy required thick skin and unwavering determination. Early in her career, she faced skepticism and resistance, with some questioning whether her unique perspective would resonate with mainstream audiences. Undeterred, she leaned into her differences, transforming potential liabilities into strengths.

Her openness about these struggles has endeared her to fans, who admire her transparency and perseverance. Through her comedy, she addresses the microaggressions and biases she has encountered, turning painful moments into powerful punchlines. In doing so, she empowers others to confront their own challenges with humor and grace.

Philosophy and Vision for the Future

At the core of Zarna's philosophy is a deep commitment to authenticity and empathy. She believes that comedy has the power to heal, unite, and provoke meaningful conversations. "Laughter," she says, "is the ultimate equalizer. It reminds us of our shared humanity, even when we feel worlds apart."

Looking ahead, Zarna envisions a future where representation is not the exception but the norm. She dreams of a world where every child grows up seeing themselves reflected in the stories they consume—a vision she works tirelessly to realize through her art and advocacy.

Her long-term goals include establishing a foundation dedicated to supporting emerging artists from underrepresented backgrounds. By providing resources, mentorship, and funding, she hopes to create a sustainable pipeline of diverse talent poised to shape the future of entertainment.

An Ever-Evolving Legacy

Zarna Garg's biography is still being written, with each chapter revealing new facets of her boundless creativity and resilience. From her humble beginnings in India to her current status as a global icon, her journey exemplifies the transformative power of courage and conviction.

What sets Zarna apart is not just her accomplishments but her willingness to evolve—to grow as an artist, a mother, a wife, and a citizen of the world. As she continues to push boundaries and inspire others, one thing is certain: Zarna Garg will leave behind a legacy defined not only by laughter but by love, compassion, and an unshakable belief in the goodness of people.

Through her relentless pursuit of excellence and her steadfast dedication to uplifting others, Zarna proves that greatness lies not in perfection but in the courage to keep reinventing oneself—and the world—through humor and heart.

The Intersection of Comedy and Social Commentary

Zarna Garg's work is more than entertainment—it's a form of social commentary that challenges audiences to think critically about the world around them. Her comedy often delves into topics like gender roles, cultural assimilation, and societal expectations, using humor as a tool to spark dialogue and inspire change. By weaving personal anecdotes with broader observations, she creates a tapestry of stories that are both intimate and universal.

One of her recurring themes is the tension between tradition and modernity, particularly within immigrant families. She tackles this with razor-sharp wit, exposing the absurdities while celebrating the beauty of navigating two worlds. Her ability to highlight contradictions without alienating her audience has made her a trusted voice in discussions about identity and belonging.

In recent years, Zarna has also addressed pressing global issues through her platform, including climate change, mental health awareness, and women's rights. While these topics might seem serious for a comedian, she approaches them with a deft touch, finding humor in even the darkest corners. This balance of levity and gravity underscores her versatility as an artist and thinker.

Collaborations and Cross-Disciplinary Projects

As Zarna continues to expand her creative horizons, she has embraced collaborations with artists from diverse disciplines. From musicians and visual artists to filmmakers and activists, she thrives on interdisciplinary projects that push the boundaries of storytelling. One such collaboration involved working with a renowned choreographer to create a multimedia performance piece that combined comedy, dance, and spoken word—a project hailed as "genre-defying" by critics.

She has also partnered with tech innovators to explore how emerging technologies can enhance storytelling. For instance, she recently experimented with virtual reality (VR) to develop an immersive experience based on her stand-up material. This cutting-edge approach allows audiences to step inside her world, experiencing her jokes and insights in a completely new way.

These ventures demonstrate Zarna's commitment to staying ahead of the curve while remaining true to her roots. Her willingness to embrace innovation ensures that her work remains fresh and relevant in an ever-changing landscape.

Advocacy Through Education

Education remains a cornerstone of Zarna's advocacy efforts. In addition to mentoring aspiring comedians and writers, she has developed educational initiatives aimed at fostering critical thinking and creativity among young people. Through workshops and curriculum development, she emphasizes the importance of storytelling as a means of self-expression and empowerment.

One notable initiative is her partnership with schools to create programs that encourage students to share their own stories. These programs focus on helping participants build confidence, hone their communication skills, and celebrate their unique perspectives. Zarna believes that storytelling is a fundamental human right—one that should be accessible to everyone, regardless of background or circumstance.

Her work in education extends beyond classrooms, as she frequently speaks at conferences and summits about the role of humor in learning and leadership. Drawing from her own experiences, she illustrates how laughter can break down barriers, foster empathy, and inspire action.

A Voice for Women Everywhere

As a woman in a field dominated by men, Zarna has consistently used her platform to amplify the voices of other women. Whether through her podcast, interviews, or live performances, she champions female empowerment and advocates for gender equality. Her humor often highlights the double standards women face, turning frustration into fuel for laughter and progress.

In 2024, she launched a special segment on The Zarna Garg Show called "Women Who Inspire," featuring interviews with trailblazing women from various industries. These conversations delve into their struggles, triumphs, and lessons learned, offering listeners a source of motivation and solidarity. The segment quickly gained popularity, further cementing Zarna's reputation as a champion of women's voices.

Her involvement in feminist causes extends to her support for organizations fighting for reproductive rights, equal pay, and access to education. She uses her influence to raise awareness and funds, ensuring that her activism matches the passion of her artistry.

The Art of Balancing Act

Behind the scenes, Zarna is a master of balance—juggling her career, family, and personal aspirations with remarkable grace. Despite her demanding schedule, she prioritizes quality time with her loved ones, viewing her relationships as the foundation of her success. Her husband, Shalabh, plays an active role in supporting her endeavors, often joining her on tour or assisting with logistics.

Her children continue to inspire much of her material, though she is careful to maintain their privacy. She credits them with teaching her valuable life lessons, many of which find their way into her routines. Their unwavering belief in her abilities gave her the courage to pursue comedy in the first place, and their pride in her achievements fuels her drive to keep pushing forward.

This delicate balancing act is something Zarna openly discusses, acknowledging the challenges of being a working mother and artist. Her honesty resonates with fans who see themselves in her struggles, making her not just a comedian but a relatable confidante.

Dreams Yet to Be Realized

While Zarna has accomplished so much, she remains driven by dreams yet unfulfilled. Among her aspirations is the creation of a television series inspired by her life—a semi-autobiographical show that captures the humor, heartache, and hilarity of growing up between cultures. She envisions the series as a celebration of resilience, blending comedy and drama to tell a story that feels both deeply personal and universally resonant.

Another goal is to establish a global comedy festival focused on amplifying underrepresented voices. Modeled after her own journey, the festival would provide a platform for emerging comedians to showcase their talents while fostering cross-cultural exchange. It's a vision rooted in her belief that comedy can bridge divides and unite people from all walks of life.

Made in United States
Cleveland, OH
13 June 2025